DEPRESSION
DEFEATED

Your Pit
Has a
Purpose

DEPRESSION
DEFEATED

Your Pit
Has a
Purpose

KELLEY STEELE

Hunter Heart Publishing
DuPont, Washington

Depression Defeated: Your Pit Has a Purpose

To order products, or for any other correspondence:

Hunter Heart Publishing
P.O. Box 354
DuPont, Washington 98327
Tel. (253) 906-2160 – Fax: (253) 912-1667
E-mail: publisher@hunterheartpublishing.com
Or reach us on the internet: www.hunterheartpublishing.com

"Offering God's Heart to a Dying World"

This book and all other Hunter Heart Publishing™ books are available at
Christian bookstores and distributors worldwide.

Chief Editor: Brenda Mates
Creative design: Phil Coles Independent Design
Cover format and logos: Exousia Marketing Group www.exousiamg.com

ISBN: 978-0-9828377-6-4

For Worldwide Distribution, Printed in the United States of America.

Dedication

Would you look at God! From finding purpose in my own pit to writing a book to help others realize their pit has a purpose. How could I have done this without my best friend and husband Reginald Steele? Thank You Lord for creating us to be one flesh; fulfilling Your will for our lives together, and "Building Your Kingdom, One Family at a Time."

How will this book help you?

This book was a product of God allowing me to see, just like Joseph, that my pit had a purpose. Read on to understand what depression is, how to identify the symptoms of depression, and that praise and powerful prayer are produced in the pit, which is ammunition to help you get out. God has a purpose and destiny for your life. Seek Him in your pit and watch God pull you out!

James 4:7-8: *"Therefore submit to God. Resist the devil and he will flee from you. [8] Draw near to God and He will draw near to you."*

Contents

Introduction

"Now Joseph had a dream, and he told it to his brothers; and they hated him even more. ^{6} So he said to them, "Please hear this dream which I have dreamed: ^{7} There we were, binding sheaves in the field. Then behold, my sheaf arose and also stood upright; and indeed your sheaves stood all around and bowed down to my sheaf."

"Now when they saw him afar off, even before he came near them, they conspired against him to kill him. ^{19} Then they said to one another, "Look, this dreamer is coming! ^{20} Come therefore, let us now kill him and cast him into some pit; and we shall say, 'Some wild beast has devoured him.' We shall see what will become of his dreams!"

Genesis 37:5-7; 18-20

How many of you know that when you share your dreams, not everyone is excited to hear them? They may listen to you, but deep in their heart, they really begin to hate you more than what they hated you before. Not for any particular reason, but just because you are dreaming. We all should believe God for something. We all should dream.

Joseph's brothers hated him, because he was a dreamer. He had purpose, he had vision, he had passion, and he was a young man of God; only seventeen at this time. And because he shared this dream of them bowing down to him, they wanted to kill him, and therefore threw him into a pit. They wanted to see what would become of his dream. Isn't it amazing that people want to put you in a pit, cast you away, talk about you, and lie on you simply because you have a dream and a vision. I don't know about you, but I know what that feels like. I am living for God and believing Him for big things, and people get angry, because I am dreaming. I have learned that most people who do this are in a pit themselves, and don't want you to get out, but to hang around in that pit with them.

Have you ever heard about the crab in the barrel theory? Anytime someone sees you rising up and stepping out, they want to pull you right back down into the pit with them, just as crabs do when one tries to get out of the barrel. We know that misery loves company; therefore, when someone sees you doing well and they are not, they will try to pull you back down into the pit with them.

All of us have been in a pit at one moment in our lives; spiritually, physically, emotionally, or mentally. When you have family situations, this could be a pit for you. For some, it is when someone turns their back on you when you need them the most. They can betray you or talk about you. Your pit can be when you lose your job. The enemy would love nothing more than to keep you in that pit, because it will cause your dream to die. When dreams die that means that you no longer have vision; you no longer have purpose and you don't even feel like living anymore. You feel like you cannot go on. We have to be careful to realize that when we are in the pit, yes, it has a purpose, because it is a starting point for God doing great things in our lives. Wherever you see someone in a pit or in a bad situation in the Bible, you know that if they continue to keep on praising, keep on worshipping, and keep on living for God, they will soon be exalted.

Many of us get stuck in the pit and never find our way out of it. Until you begin to understand the purpose of why you are in the pit, you will never get out of it. To be released into our full ministry capacity, no matter to what extent that may be, we all need to go through a pit experience. I believe that we need to be able to understand the purpose of such an experience to be able to overcome it. If you can understand how your enemy works, you can battle it easier. We need to understand that pits can become enemies in our lives. If we refuse to come out of this pit, our purpose will not manifest.

My Pit of Depression

I had been a leader in ministry for several years before I found myself battling depression. I always considered myself a strong and positive woman. I was the type of person who saw the glass half full, never half empty. But after years of dealing with the typical issues of life, I allowed myself to accept the fact that life was just hard. And the best way to deal with the hard times of life was to give up on living. It somehow became easier to be hopeless, because if I expected the worst, I would not have to deal with the potential let down.

It was one incident in particular that occurred early on in ministry when I found myself in a pit of depression. As a Pastor's wife, I knew how to deal with the ups and downs of leading a church. I understood that in ministry, people come and people go. I accepted the truth of my calling; that it was a job that deals directly with people and their issues. But one particular year, I found myself dealing with direct hits from those who I felt were closest to me. People that I labored with in church somehow turned from those I considered friends to enemies. Instead of praying to God to help me deal with the loss of those I had grown to love, I began to believe the voice in my head; that I had done something wrong, that I was not worthy to have friends, or that I could not trust anyone who came into my life. I began to isolate myself from others, and soon, I was at church, but refusing to embrace the people in the church and slowly embraced depression instead.

During my own personal study to help others, I had learned over 30 million people in the United States deal with depression. And here I was a leader of a great church, married to a great man of God and a mother of wonderful children moving into what I call the "pit of depression". I would walk into church like everything was okay, but cry the entire drive home from service hating the lie I was living. As months went by, I found myself feeling like it was okay to live in my pit. Although I believed the best for others, I truly did not see better for myself. I convinced my heart that I belonged in the pit; that I was better away from those I loved. I slowly forgot that God desired my life to be free in Him. And that's what happens in the pit of depression. Your memory of the Word of God that has been written on your heart eventually fades in the darkness.

At first, I was able to cope with life for most of the day, but I would long for the night to come so I could just sleep. As time went on, I changed from a woman who viewed sleeping during the day as a waste of time to one who would desperately need a nap a few hours after waking up in the morning. Those short naps would sometimes become hours and at times, I would sleep the day away. I would cancel scheduled appointments and miss events for my kids just to hide away in my bed. I would put myself in a coma by turning off the phone, shutting all of the window shades, putting on blinders and earplugs to shut the world away. I would fall asleep praying that the heaviness would be gone when I woke up. But there it would be; a spirit of heaviness ready to greet me, and I would reluctantly put it on.

Not only did I sleep a lot in my pit, but I ate a lot too. I used food to medicate the pain I was feeling. Food was the temporary highlight of my day. The preparing of it, the taste of it, the full and comforted feeling after eating it; and then the guilt would come. Why did I eat so much? Why could I just not stop? Why would I put fattening, sugar-filled treats into my body day after day, knowing it was bad for me? And then the condemnation would come when I looked into the mirror, as the pounds began to pack on. Then, I burrowed further into my pit because I hated who I was: an overweight, sad, disconnected, lying preacher who encouraged strangers to live while personally, privately wanting to die.

At my lowest point, I accepted that my life would always be like this- dull, lonely, and dark. My husband and my children would ask me what was wrong, and I simply answered I was just going through a tough time. But in reality, I convinced myself I would always live in this pit. I had begun to fight off thoughts of suicide when my mom confronted me.

It was before church one hot August evening. I was sitting at my desk in my office, trying to gather myself together before presenting a message before the members of our church. I can still remember how hard it was to open my eyes to read my notes, because they felt so heavy. My husband came to me and prayed for me. I tried to receive the prayer, but I just honestly didn't care anymore. I said amen just to end with agreement, but truly did not agree with the life he had spoken over me. Suddenly, out of the blue, my mom comes into the office. She made me look at her square in the eyes and asked me what was wrong. I lied and said nothing. She quickly reminded me she was my mother and knew something was wrong. Then, she said she was tired of seeing me sad and reminded me I had a responsibility to lead, teach, give, and live. She encouraged me to get up.

Something clicked that evening. I'm not sure if I realized my façde could no longer be hidden from others or if my soul was open to the voice of my mom, or if I had finally allowed the truth of God to flood my heart. Whatever the reason, I finally found the strength to live and love again; I found the strength to get out of the pit. I began to believe with Christ, I could do all things, and that depression could be defeated!

The clinical definition of depression is simply to be spiritually pressed down. It is amazing how the medical world sees depression as a spiritual issue. In the 21st century, they have tried to place all kinds of labels on it and call it different names, saying it is genetic, which it may be in some cases, but it can be generational curses. You may have the medical symptoms the doctor has diagnosed you with, but in actuality, it is a spiritual condition. Please understand, if you have been diagnosed with depression by a physician, I am by no means advising you to go home and stop taking medication that has been prescribed to you. But I do believe once you align the Word of God in your life, you can trust that God is able to set you free from being dependent upon medication that is keeping you regulated.

Remember, I lived in a pit, so I know what it is like to not want to get up and take care of yourself. I know what it is like to lay in bed and hide under the covers. I know what it is like to want to eat and eat and eat to drown the pain that you have inside of you. Then, you lay in bed all day crying, because you feel guilty about what you just ate. You feel big and heavy and that no one loves you. I know what a hopeless, pressed down life feels like. And I have to be honest, for awhile, it felt good to be in the pit. It felt good to shut off life and not be responsible for anything.

When you are depressed, it means you lose your ability to feel; you don't care what happens in your life. When you are depressed, you just feel numb. You are not really happy or sad; you are just in a low place. When you don't have your emotions working the way God designed for them to work, you will not know how to praise God when something good happens for someone else. It's a blessing to feel good when something is going to happen. It's a blessing to feel joy when you walk into the house of God. It's a blessing to feel angry at sin, or when you see someone overtaken by the enemy. It is a blessing to know God has your back and that you are living for a purpose. Our relationships are all tied up in emotions. If you refuse to feel, you refuse to feel for others. And if you do not care for yourself, you cannot feel for others. The Word of God instructs us to love our neighbor as ourselves, but if you can't connect emotionally, it is impossible to feel love for anyone. It's all based upon emotions, and if you allow depression to keep your feelings suppressed, your relationship with Christ will dwindle away.

Depression almost had its way with me. I almost gave into the lie that I would always have a spirit of heaviness to combat. I almost accepted that my place in life was to live in the pit. But by the grace of God, I have escaped the pit of depression. I allowed the Word of God to be a ladder in my soul. I had to choose every day what I was going to serve; the depression that waited to greet me every morning, or the new mercy God had prepared for me at the rising of the sun. I accepted the truth that depression was trying to become a stronghold in my life, rooted in disappointment and girded by the unwillingness to forgive those who I felt had hurt me. And because God loves us all the same, He can get you out of your pit, as He did for me.

Symptoms of Depression

Restlessness

One cause of depression is restlessness. Restlessness causes you to feel uneasy. It causes your mind not to rest and ultimately causes you to be unable to relax. God desires that we live a life of leisure in Him.

"Therefore, since a promise remains of entering His rest, let us fear lest any of you seem to have come short of it."

Hebrews 4:1

God has promised us rest and desires that we enter into His rest. Because we have to enter into it tells me a choice has to be made. The door that leads to rest is open, so you have to walk to get to it. In other words, you have to get up and make an effort to find your promised rest. If you make a choice not to walk into His rest, you possibly have made a choice to live a life of worry, or a restless life.

The Bible tells us that worry is a sin.

"...for whatever is not from faith is sin..."

Romans 14:23

Restlessness, or worry, is a type of fear that is completely opposite of faith. A Christian life is lived based upon faith. If you are living a life of faith, you cannot be living a life of fear. It is hot or cold, black or white, up or down; there is no in between when it comes to faith. It is either one or the other. At times, I believe the enemy tries to keep us from what God has for us by causing us to waver back and forth between the two.

"Be anxious for nothing..."

Philippians 4:6

When you worry and do not believe God at His Word, you are living a sinful life. I used to worry that I had nothing to worry about! I would worry about everything. I used to think if I worried enough, something would change. I thought there was some kind of system that would calculate how much I worried, and just somehow it would fix my situations, but it is a trick of the enemy. Satan knows if he can get you to worry just a little, he can get you to step out of that faith realm.

Even in the pit, when it looks like things are going crazy, and when you don't even understand what is going on, you must not worry. We are called to walk by faith and not by sight. I know when we are in a pit, it is a pretty dark place, but be encouraged, because it is not about what we see anyway. It is about the faith inside of you and knowing and believing God's Word over that situation. In the Kingdom, we have to believe before we see. I need for you to believe that God is going to make a way of escape out of that pit. It will not always be like this; it will not always be this dark, it will not always be this cold, you will not always be alone, and you have got to believe it before you see it!

It is in the pit where your faith must arise to get you out of your situation. So refuse to live a restless life, and exercise your faith in God.

Fatigue & Lack of Energy

The pit can also produce fatigue and a lack of energy. Fatigue means weariness or exhaustion from labor, exertion, or stress. You get tired when you are stressed out. It is an exhausting experience when you are in the pit, because when you begin to try to figure out how God is going to work it out, you take on a role that is not yours to take. You are not the King of kings and you are not the Lord of lords. I used to be one of those people who would get up in the middle of the night and pick up all of the bills and write down what I owed, and add and subtract from my bank account. I would go back and do it on a calculator and still come up with the same numbers. It was exhausting! I woke up in the morning even more tired, because I sat up all night doing this.

One day, I decided I was not going to live like this. I chose to step into the faith realm and made a choice to be still and know that He was God. I learned how to wait on the Lord. When we learn how to wait on the Lord and stop worrying; all of a sudden, we are no longer tired and exhausted anymore. I have learned in the Kingdom that it is sometimes best to do nothing. When you choose to wait, God will step in and do something.

"But those who wait on the LORD shall renew their strength; They shall mount up with wings like eagles, They shall run and not be weary, They shall walk and not faint."

Isaiah 40:31

Just wait on the Lord! Stop thinking, stop calculating, stop trying to figure it out, and all of a sudden, you will begin to feel a strength that you have never felt before! Things will begin to turn inside of your spirit and you will no longer be exhausted; you will no longer be tired, and you will not be stressed out any more. Your strength will be renewed! You will do as the Word says and mount up with wings as eagles. This means you will be able to go higher and see further into your situations, because God has made a way for you. It also says you shall run and not be weary. God will give us the strength to get up out of that "pit mentality" and run and praise Him, and not become tired or weary while we are going through the process. We can praise Him in it knowing that He is bringing us out of it! It also says we will walk and not faint. It is not time for us to lie down and die. It is not time for us to faint. It is not time for us to take a break. It is not time for us to take a nap. Wake up in the name of Jesus. Stop worrying! It's something about waiting; it's something about being still; it's something about taking a step back and saying, "God, I am going to let you be God in this situation." It might take longer than you want it to take. It might hurt more than you expected it to hurt, but just step back and let Jesus do what He does best. When you do, your strength will come.

Hopelessness & Helplessness

Another aspect that we must deal with when it comes to the pit of depression is hopelessness and helplessness. Hopelessness is where you have no expectation of good in your life, or obtaining success. If you have ever talked to a hopeless person, no matter what you do or say; no matter what scripture you give or what song you sing to them; no matter what tape, CD or DVD you give to them, they are so hopeless that they don't even want to hear what you have to say. You try your best to give them what the Word says and encourage them through your own experiences, but many of them refuse to receive what you are giving them and want to stay in their pit. Why? Because they feel like it takes too much work to get out of the pit. They would rather sit in the pit and feel sorry about themselves, instead of pulling themselves up out of there.

You need to cut yourself off from people who refuse to come out of those situations. You move forward and let them know that when they decide to come up out of that pit, you will be there for them, but you cannot stay in there with them. You cannot pity people who are in these situations. You have done all that you can do. You have dropped the ladder down for them, but they do not want to climb up. Just leave it there for them and walk away. When people cannot expect good for their lives, how do you think that they are going to rejoice with you when good things happen in your life? Didn't Joseph's brothers hate his dream? They did not have any expectation of good in their own lives, so they could not receive the good that was about to happen in his life.

Helplessness means lack of protection and support. You have to have hope as a confident expectation that God is going to move in your life. Hope is so important that Romans 8:24-25 says,

"For we were saved in this hope, but hope that is seen is not hope; for why does one still hope for what he sees? 25 But if we hope for what we do not see, we eagerly wait for it with perseverance."

Look at it like this. I cannot hope I am in a church if I am already in a church; that is not hope, but a reality. But I can hope for us to be in a 5000 seat church, because we are not yet there. This is future tense. I don't see it, but I can still hope. The pits purpose is to cause you to never hope again. Be encouraged, because in the pit, you are hoping for better things to happen. You are not helpless. It is a lie from the enemy that tells us that there is no help during these pit experiences. It is in these pits; these dark, cold, and lonely places where we begin to cry out seeking God. The enemy wants you to doubt God and to doubt His presence.

"Our soul waits for the LORD; He is our help and our shield."

Psalm 33:20

We have to allow our soul and emotions to wait on the Lord. We cannot just freak out when situations turn in another direction than what we expected. We have to put those emotions, our soul, in check and wait on the Lord, so that He can be our shield. Psalm 46:1 says God is our refuge and strength; a very present help in trouble. This should bless many of us right now. If you are in trouble of any sort, the Word says that He is a very present help in those times. When you feel like you have no idea how things are going to work out and you feel like the whole world is collapsing around you, you have to know that God is with you. God is not afraid of trouble. He actually shows up in trouble. So if you are having trouble in your life, you need to give God praise right now, and thank Him, because He is right there with you in the middle of the mess! God is good!

I hear people say that they cannot feel God or that He is nowhere to be found, but if you would just stop worrying and stop toiling and lift your hands up and worship Him, you will see that He is right there with you. He will never leave you nor forsake you. He will never leave you by yourself. He is not a man that He should lie; He is right there with you in the middle of your hell!

"Unless the LORD had been my help, My soul would soon have settled in silence."

Psalm 94:17

Isn't that what happens when you are in a pit and depressed? Your soul sits in silence. Your emotions are cut off and you cannot feel anymore, but the psalmist said that the Lord was his help and this is why he made it through. If He did it for him, He can do it for you. He did it for me, so He will also do it for you. If He did it once, He will do it again.

Worthlessness

The pit is a very hard place to be and satan wants nothing more than to keep us there by any means. Worthlessness means lacking meaning and value; feeling useless. Many people who enter the pit of depression begin to drink or hurt themselves, because they feel they have no value, no meaning in life. Some drink, some do drugs, and some overeat, because they feel worthless. If you value yourself, you will not want to put any kind of poison into your body. When you value yourself, you do not want to put yourself in harm's way.

The fact that you are being picked on by the enemy is proof that you are valuable. Genesis 1:26-27:

"Then God said, "Let Us make man in Our image, according to Our likeness; let them have dominion over the fish of the sea, over the birds of the air, and over the cattle, over all the earth and over every creeping thing that creeps on the earth." [27] So God created man in His own image; in the image of God He created him; male and female He created them."

If you ever feel that you are not valuable, you need to look in the mirror and tell God that He must be attractive, because He made you to look just like Him. Don't think that this is strange. Whatever it takes to let you know how valuable you are to God, you need to do it. You have to know who you are and what God thinks of you, and how He created you to be.

"For You formed my inward parts; You covered me in my mother's womb.[14] I will praise You, for I am fearfully and wonderfully made; Marvelous are Your works, And that my soul knows very well. [15] My frame was not hidden from You, When I was made in secret, And skillfully wrought in the lowest parts of the earth [16] Your eyes saw my substance, being yet unformed. And in Your book they all were written, The days fashioned for me, When as yet there were none of them."

Psalm 139:13-16

When you are in the pit and satan is telling you that you are no good; that you look funny, and that no one wants to be around you, you're weird, your hips are too big, your lips are too big, your nose is too big, or whatever lie the enemy tries to conjure up to you, you need to remind yourself that you are fearfully and wonderfully made.

The reason why I talk the way I do is because God knew I was going to use my voice to speak to other people. Or the reason I think the way I do is because God was going to use my mind to advance His Kingdom. And the reason why I like to be organized is because God knew I was going to be very sharp and shrewd and business-like in this world for the Kingdom. Stop doubting yourself and denying yourself and know that you are fearfully and wonderfully made. Ephesians 1:4 says, "just as He chose us in Him before the foundation of the world, that we should be holy and without blame before Him in love."

"In Him you also trusted, after you heard the word of truth, the gospel of your salvation; in whom also, having believed, you were sealed with the Holy Spirit of promise, [14] who is the guarantee of our inheritance until the redemption of the purchased possession, to the praise of His glory."

Ephesians 1:13-14

We were purchased; we were chosen by God Himself. Even while you are in the pit, you must know that you were chosen by God. Even when you are by yourself and feel alone, you were chosen. Even when you feel like dying, you have to know that you were chosen. Even when you have no hope and feel like giving up, you have to know that you were chosen. There is a reason why you are in this pit, but God has a set time to get you out. Be still and know that He is God.

Withdrawal

Another symptom of depression is withdrawal. The process of withdrawal does not occur overnight. It is a gradual moving away, or pulling away from people, places, and things you usually love. When you withdraw, you retire, retreat and eventually detach from social or emotional involvement.

To retire means to stop working. Wouldn't it be the enemies plan to get you to a place where you stopped working? The Bible explains the importance of continuing to work in the book of John 9:4:

"I must work the works of Him who sent Me while it is day, for the night is coming when no one can work."

Although this is Jesus explaining to the disciples the assignment on His life and that His time on earth would be limited, we as Christians should have the same thoughts. We are alive for a limited amount of time. That time is precious and valuable not only to those around us, but to the Lord. Just like Jesus, we too must work the works; the good works of being salt and light in the earth.

When depression knocks on your heart, you no longer want to take the time to season anyone else's life, and you surely don't want to allow your light to shine. That light usually becomes dim with despair, and when you stop working to add flavor to others, or to point people to the direction of the Son, you have retired.

Retiring and retreating have similar definitions, but retreating is a word used more in a military battle or in warfare. In 2 Timothy 2:3, the Word of God instructs us to, *"...endure hardship as a good soldier of Jesus Christ."* To endure means to continue on even in the midst of trouble. But typically, its trouble that got you into your pit in the first place; the pit becomes a place of false protection or shelter. Because you have hidden yourself in a dark place, you eventually begin to emotionally and socially detach from those you love or the things you once loved to do. When you begin to stop loving people, you ultimately stop loving God.

Matthew 22:37-39 instructs us to *"....love the Lord your God with all your heart, with all your soul, and with all your mind. This is the first and great commandment. And the second is like it: 'You shall love your neighbor as yourself.'"*

To love means to show great affection for. Jesus teaches us that we have to love the Lord with all of our heart. According to Proverbs 4:23, your heart determines the course of your life (NLT). Your heart is what drives you to love, to pursue and to excel. Your heart produces passion and endurance. It is when your heart is grieved by loss, disappointment, or by letdown, that blood-pumping passion can easily turn into a sluggish, silent beat. Lack of heart affects your soul, which is the seat of your emotions. If your heart is barely beating, your emotions will be dull. Additionally, your lack of emotions affects your mind to think clearly and to recall the truth of the love that God has for you and the love you have for God. If you don't love God, you will stop loving others, and eventually yourself.

When I was in my pit, I remember when withdrawal set in on my life. It started after I felt wounded by a close friend who served with me in ministry. It's one thing to get hurt by someone expected to cut you off, but when it is someone you love as a dear friend, it is another situation. When the relationship ended, I began to not only guard my heart, but cut it off completely. I had made up in my mind that I would not put myself in harm's way anymore by refusing to give my entire heart to anything. This included what I loved to do; teach the Word of God at church.

Eventually, I stopped going to my women's events at church. Then, I cancelled the events completely. I started going to my room and living in a dark shell where I felt protected. I began to stop calling my mom and my sister on a daily basis to communicate, and started to no longer communicate with my family. It wasn't long after, I stopped communicating with Jesus through prayer. Ultimately, my love for people left, my love for God withered away, and I slowly began to hate myself. Surely something was wrong with me, look at all the people who had cut me off - no, correction, that I had cut off. Soon, I purposely found reasons to miss church completely. My pit had become my church.

Hebrews 10:25 says, *"not forsaking the assembling of ourselves together as is the manner of some, but exhorting one another, and so much the more as you see the Day approaching."*

When you withdraw yourself from church, you do exactly what the Word of God tells you not to do. Do not forsake (turn away from, reject) the assembling (coming together as one) together - or in basic terms, do not stop going to church. There is power and strength found when you come together as a body of believers. Exhortation occurs; encouragement and lifting up, by speaking life (the Word of God) to one another.

Instead of retreating, retiring or shutting off, you have to press even the more to continue to do the things you love–especially loving others. When you love others, you love yourself, and if you love yourself, you love the God who created you.

Thoughts of Death

Ultimately, the pit produces thoughts of death. When you are depressed, alone, and feel like you are never going to get out of that pit, and like it is too much to handle, the enemy will whisper in your ear to end your life. He will tell you to end your life, that no one will miss you, and that you can let go and rest in Heaven with the Lord. The devil is a liar! God knows the number of days in your life. He knows how long you are supposed to be here; we don't determine that. This is a touchy subject, but suicide IS NOT an option. If you are dealing with that you better rebuke that in the name of Jesus. That IS NOT of God! You have a reason to be on this Earth. I don't care how bad you think it is, at least you can open up your eyes and look up at the blue sky and say, "God, I may be going through a pit experience, but at least I can see you, and I have another day to face." You cannot die!

"I shall not die, but live, And declare the works of the LORD."

Psalm 118:17

David declared this statement when he was in a pit situation. He had to remind himself and tell himself that he would not die. You need to be able to speak to yourself and your circumstances while you are going through your pit experiences, so that you can pull yourself up, just as David did. As I said before, the enemy is here to kill your dreams and stop the purposes that you were placed on this Earth to accomplish.

Symptoms of Depression Summary

I know it may feel good at times to be in a pit. You feel like you just want to shut the blinds, turn off the lights, cut off the phone, get in the bed, and cut yourself off from the entire outside world. It is easy and feels good, because you no longer have to try or work at anything. You just give up, but I am here to tell you that you were not designed to stay in a pit. The pit will produce two things in your life: it will either produce you to be pitiful, or it will produce you to be powerful. Remember, the pit causes restlessness; it causes you to be anxious, causes you to worry, and you are not even able to relax, because you are not sure what God is going to do. We have to realize when we worry, we are sinning. You might not have committed adultery, fornicated, smoked, or gone to the bars, and you may have watched all of the right things, but if you are a worrier, you are sinning according to the Word of God. The reason it is a sin is because you are either fearful, or you are faithful. There is no in between. There is no gray area in this thing.

The reason satan loves to keep us going back and forth between fear and faith is because he understands if he can keep us in the realm of fear long enough, we will miss the blessing, and if we miss the blessing, we will begin to doubt God and not trust or have hope that He will come through for us. But it is not God's fault that you missed it, because you were in the wrong place. We have to be in the place of faith at all times. According to Ephesians 2:8, we are saved by faith. A seed of faith was placed inside of you by the preacher, or by your grandmother, or someone who spoke life over you, and this led you to desire salvation. When you became saved, something happened. You did not see that you were saved, but you knew that you were born again, that you were adopted, and that Jesus loved you. This is how faith begins, and then we see in James 5:15 that the prayer of faith will save the sick. We have prayed over people with cancer and diseases and believed that they were healed and well, but they too must believe the Word of God for their own lives as well.

"But let him ask in faith, with no doubting, for he who doubts is like a wave of the sea driven and tossed by the wind."

James 1:6

It says that if we do not ask in faith, we will have nothing; we will not have anything from God. If you go up to be healed, and someone prays over you, if you leave with doubt in your heart, you will not receive your healing.

"But he who doubts is condemned if he eats, because he does not eat from faith; for whatever is not from faith is sin."

Romans 14:23

So we have to be sure not to live in the place of restlessness, but in the place of faith. When you are in a pit by yourself and it is dark and you are alone, and those who you trusted put you in there, it is very easy to worry and wonder how God is going to get you out, or how He is going to make things better. I encourage you today to not stay in that place, but pull yourself up out of that realm. Worry is a tool of satan, and if he can get you to that place, you will begin to work on his behalf, but I want you to be free today! Come up out of that pit of worry.

The second thing we discussed was that the pit will produce fatigue or lack of energy. When you are in a pit you feel tired. You try to figure out how things are going to change; you try to figure out how things are going to get better; you try to work out a plan in the middle of the night and you allow yourself to stay up all night. You wake up the next morning just as tired, if not more, than before you went to sleep. As I said before, I used to literally sit up all night adding up my bills; adding and subtracting and multiplying and dividing to come up with the right numbers. I would go over it again with a calculator just to get the same number, multiplying and long division thinking I would come up with a different number. I would worry all night long, and wake up exhausted from the night before. I have learned in life that the best thing to do when you are in a pit situation; when you can't make any difference and when it seems like it is not getting any better, don't do ANYTHING!

I cannot explain it, but something happens when you decide to be still and not do anything. I am not talking about lying down and dying. I am talking about when you stop thinking about your situation; when you stop worrying about how God is going to get you through or how He is going to get you out. Be still and know that God is God. You begin to apply the Word of God to your life, and you say, "Okay God, I don't understand it, but I know I am in this pit and even though I don't know how to get out or how long I will be in here, I do know it will not be forever. I believe t if I stand still and trust in Your Word, you will give me strength to come out of here."

"But those who wait on the LORD shall renew their strength; they shall mount up with wings like eagles, they shall run and not be weary, they shall walk and not faint."

Isaiah 40:31

See, it's something about waiting upon the Lord. If we could just grab a hold of this thing people of God, and learn instead of worrying and being tired, to wait on God, our strength will be renewed. I don't know how it works. I don't know how it happens, but all of sudden, when you give up fighting, and you stand still in the middle of your pit and say, "God, I give You my issues. I give You my problems. I give You my finances. I give You my marriage. I give You my children. I give You my sickness. I give You my home. I give You my job. I give You my car. I give You my mental state. I give You my heart condition. I give You my soul. God, when I give You all of this and be still before You, my strength is renewed!" And guess what? You are about to mount up with wings as eagles, and the Word of God says you will run and not be weary; you will walk and not faint! Just be still and your strength will be renewed. Hallelujah!

Stop running around in the pit. Do you realize if you keep running around, you are digging yourself deeper into that pit? If you just be still, it is only a matter of time before God will lift you out.

Another product of the pit is hopelessness. Hopeless people will not receive anything from you.

You can give them a Word or a testimony, and at the end of it, you feel like you have hit a home run and that they are going to come out of that thing, but they turn around and say, "Well, you don't know what I am going through." They say things are not going to get better and things are not going to change, but that is a lie from the pit of hell. Being hopeful means to have a confident expectation of something. You have to be confident in expecting, even in your pit. It's easy to be confident when you are walking around and everything is going good, but you must maintain that confidence even while in the pit. Everything around may look contrary to what you believe God for, but you must know you are coming out; you must have a firm assurance.

There is something about remaining firm and hopeful while you are in a pit.

"And not only that, but we also glory in tribulations, knowing that tribulation produces perseverance."

Romans 5:3

This literally means to rejoice in time of trouble. When you are in the middle of a pit, and things do not look like they are going your way, and you are having a hard time and feeling a spirit of depression, you must be able to flip this thing around and see it as God trying to get something out of you during this situation. He is trying to do something with your heart. You are developing perseverance, meaning that you are not a quitter. You also develop character and experience as well. If you want to know the character of someone, squeeze on them a little bit; bump them the wrong way. Don't believe people when they say they have good character. These are just words. Rub them the wrong way, and you will see what comes out of them; the lack thereof, or plenty. Correct someone and see what comes out of them. Go ahead and tell someone about themselves, in love, and see how their character stands. It is amazing what you will find out about a person.

You have to remain hopeful. When you are in that pit, you can become or feel helpless. It is dark in there. It is cold in there, and it may seem that all hope is gone, but the devil is a liar! God is with us and He helps us.

"Our soul waits for the LORD; He is our help and our shield."

Psalms 33:20

If we could just get our emotions to wait on the Lord, we would be in a good place. If your emotions begin to rise up in your pit experience, make them wait on the Lord.

"God is our refuge and strength, A very present help in trouble."
Psalm 46:1

Is there any of you who are in trouble today? We all will face troubles in this life, and God is right there in that pit with us. This should give us excitement to know that the moment we hit trouble, God is going to

31

show up. He is a very present help. He does not wait or hang around to see how you are going to do, but there is something about our God that shows up in times of trouble. That is where He shines! He comes into our lives as a very present help.

When you are in these pits, you feel worthless, or invaluable. The enemy will lie to you and tell you that no one likes you and you are worthless. When you feel this way, you begin to do things to harm yourself. You may begin to overeat, drink, take drugs, and other things to harm yourself. Some people even cut themselves, because of feelings of worthlessness. They believe they will experience some kind of relief from doing this, but this is not the truth. As you begin to stay in the Word of God, even though you enter a pit, you understand that you will not always be there. You will be able to love yourself, even while in the pit. I have realized most women who find themselves down in the dumps, this is when God wants you to realize who you are in Him.

"Then God said, "Let Us make man in Our image, according to Our likeness; let them have dominion over the fish of the sea, over the birds of the air, and over the cattle, over all the earth and over every creeping thing that creeps on the earth."

Genesis 1:26

We need to get up in the morning and look in the mirror and say, "Wow God, I am made in Your image and in Your likeness, and I like what I see." You need to speak life to yourself. If you do not like you, who else is going to?

"For You formed my inward parts; You covered me in my mother's womb. I will praise You, for I am fearfully and wonderfully made. Marvelous are Your works, And that my soul knows very well. My frame was not hidden from You, When I was made in secret, And skillfully wrought in the lowest parts of the earth. Your eyes saw my substance, being yet unformed. And in Your book they all were written, The days fashioned for me, When as yet there were none of them."

Psalm 139:16

When you find yourself in a pit situation, you must tell yourself you are fearfully and wonderfully made. God knew everything about you. He loves everything about you, and because He loves who you are, you love who you are. Stop complaining about your lips being too big, your nose being too wide, your thighs being too big, or your hips being too wide. Listen, love who you are. Depression begins to set in, especially for those who overeat. Because you feel bad about yourself, you look in the mirror and hate what you see and begin to eat more. Instead of going to the gym, you go to the refrigerator. It is a trick of satan.

"just as He chose us in Him before the foundation of the world, that we should be holy and without blame before Him in love."

Ephesians 1:4

The pit produces prayer in our lives. When you begin to pray in the pit, it is amazing how God begins to respond to you. When you are in a pit of depression, you not only cut off the natural world around you, but you also cut off ties with God. You cannot tell me you can cut off everyone in your life and still have a relationship with God; it is not going to happen. Prayer is a form of communication. The same way you talk to your family, friends, or co-workers in the natural, prayer is that communication to Jesus in the Supernatural.

Prayer is how you get a response from Heaven. When you begin to open up your mouth and talk to God, He will hear you and help you. You may be going through, but you realize you cannot complain or worry, but trust in Him and develop your character while you are in there, so that you can come out victorious. You will develop thanksgiving in your heart, as you wait on the Lord. When you pray in the pit, you do not care how long you stay there, as long as you know you are coming out of it. As a matter of fact, when you are in the pit, it is a place of solitude away from the world. You don't have to worry about others pulling you out of your prayer time. So please enjoy that quiet time in your pit developing your relationship with God.

What Depression Produces

The Spiritual Benefits of the Pit

Praise

The first benefit of the pit is the development of your praise. I have learned that everything in the Kingdom of God is backwards. In order to increase, you have to decrease, according to John 3:30. If I want to receive, I have to give according to Luke 6:38. Using that same principal, I realized t in order to get out of a depressed state; I have to praise God at the bottom of the pit. To praise God means to have a joyful expression and adoration toward the Lord. Remember earlier, I explained that depression numbs your feelings. When you push past your emotions and dare to find them again, you can begin to express your love, admiration and gratefulness to Jesus again. In Kingdom reality, the pit can be used to develop praise once you realize there is no other way to come up out of darkness and into His marvelous light. Praising God at the bottom has a way of thrusting you to the top of whatever situation you are in. And when you are elevated higher, you can see more clearly, and the dead-end vision that tried to wrap itself around you is left behind as you rise up in Him.

Even now when depression tries to stop by and visit me, I have (by the grace of God) trained my mind to immediately begin to thank God for all that He has done for me. I start to open my mouth and show gratitude for His loving-kindness. I speak to my Father and remind Him, and myself, just how good He is.

Psalm 40:2-3 reminds us of this truth. It says, *"He brought me up also out of a horrible pit...and He has put a new song in my mouth, Praise unto our God."* There is power praising the Lord in the pit!

And when you do that, instead of thoughts of death entering into your mind, you need to allow the pit to produce praise, a fruitful prayer life, and purpose. Praise is a powerful tool against the enemy and his tactics to keep us in the pit of depression. It might just start as a quiet praise; a silent praise in your heart. Then, you begin to see your situation change, and before you know it, you don't even care you are in the pit anymore; all you care about is praising your King. You might be in that pit by yourself, but be encouraged, He is right there with you! Do you realize when you praise God; you magnify Him above that situation? This means you blow Him up bigger than all of the problems that you are facing. When we exalt God, we lift Him higher than what we are going through, and we tell the devil that the issues are small compared to the big God we serve. And because you are a child of God, you can also be exalted up with Him, leaving those problems down in that pit where they belong.

A Powerful Prayer Life

The next benefit of the pit is the development of a powerful prayer life. There is something great that transpires when praying in the pit. I have had some of my best personal prayer times in the pit when I did not know how I was going to get out, why I was there, and just asking God what I did to get there. It is in these times of great trials that our prayers become great and intense acts of worship towards our Father. It just seems as if they get answered more quickly when in the pit. In times of great worship, we lift our hands to God and some pray in this manner to God. A great example is when our young infants or toddlers lift their hands up and want you to pick them up, because they cannot do something. This is the same way we are extending our hands in worshipful prayer to God. We are asking Him to pick us up and get us out of the situations we are in. We are telling Him we need Him and surrendering our will to His will. We need to lift up our hands in the church. Some churches don't believe it is necessary, but it is absolutely necessary.

When you push forth that praise to God in the midst of your pit, and lift your hands up in worshipful prayer, letting God know you need Him, you are then ready to allow the pit experience to produce purpose in your life. It is in these pits where we are shaped and molded; where things are taken out of us, and where things are placed inside of us. If we do not allow these things to take place, then we will not come up out of these pits and our purpose will not be fulfilled. We need to be in the pit, but we must also know how to work our way out of it, so that we can do the entirety of what God has called us to in this Earth.

We have all been put into pits. Maybe not physically like Joseph, but we have been in pits that are spiritual, emotional, and mental where we feel that we have been betrayed, or where we feel that someone has broken our trust in them, or when a person close to us has pushed us into a pit like Joseph's brothers did to him.

In order for us to fulfill destiny, we cannot live in this state. Certain issues in our lives can lead to these pit experiences, including financial issues, marital issues, and family issues that will just bog you down. We must remember that the purpose of the pit was designed to kill you. It was not placed there for you to have a good time, or to vacate; it was designed to ultimately kill who you are. If not physically; it was created to kill you mentally, emotionally, socially and spiritually. It is designed to cut off your vision. If you do not have vision in the pit, you will not have purpose in order to get out and fulfill your destiny. You were not placed here to have fun; you were placed here to fulfill your purpose in life. And we must know it is not always about what we want our purpose to be, but what God ultimately wants to do through us. If we refuse to come out of this pit, our purpose will not manifest.

Depression is a self-made prison that 30 million Americans suffer with every day. I really want to deal with this spirit that is attacking the people of God. Remember, the definition means to be spiritually pressed down. We must understand it is a very real issue in our world, and I would never advise you to stop taking medications if you have been diagnosed with depression or other related illnesses, but what I do want you to do, is supplement those medications with the Word of God, so that He can wean you off in due time.

If it were not for the blood of Jesus; if it were not for the Word of God over my life; if it were not for the relationship I had with Jesus Christ, I too would be on medication for depression. I understand what it feels like to be pressed down. I understand what it feels like to be emotionally disconnected. Please do not think I am writing to you from something I have read from someone else. I have lived this thing, and I know what it feels like to think you cannot go on another day. You don't want to get out of bed, you don't want to sing, you don't want to shout, and you don't want to have any type of relationship with anyone. But because I have been set free from this spirit, I can boldly come before you to let you know that the Word of God works, and if you apply it over your life, you can have that stronghold of depression destroyed!

When someone is going through depression, they become emotionally disconnected, as we spoke about earlier. We need emotions in our lives. We need to feel happy, sad, mad and glad. We need to have an emotional relationship with others, as well as with our

Lord and Savior, Jesus Christ. You should feel excited when you know the Lord is going to do good things in your life. You should feel happy when He shows up in your life. You should feel anticipation for God to do great things. You should feel anger when sin is all around you. These are all emotions God has given to us, and we have to realize that if we lose all ability to feel in the natural, you will absolutely lose your ability to feel emotions in the supernatural. So therefore, you can't trust in God and hope for Him to do great things. You are unable to believe God, because you cannot feel anything emotionally.

I am tired of the enemy telling us that we do not have enough, or that we need to stay in some kind of low place to be Christians. I am here to tell you today that you are too blessed to be depressed! Stop saying that you are depressed; stop speaking that over your life. You have to break that confession by saying that you are joyful, you are hopeful, and that God has great things in store for your life. Stop putting a label on your forehead that says "depression". Begin to confess God has loosed you from that spirit in the name of Jesus! It may sound simple, but I am here to tell you that death and life are in the power of the tongue. (Proverbs 18:21) If you begin to speak life over you, and death to depression while developing your prayer life, all of sudden, you will feel as if you are able to rise up out of that pit.

Purpose

The last thing the pit of depression produces is your purpose. The pit is a starting block for you going into your destiny, but you must know when to come out of there, so you can get to your purpose. Don't sit around bragging that God has placed you in a pit. How long have you been there? How long are you allowing that prison to keep you bound and down and not moving into the things of God? It is a "pit-stop"; only for a moment, to get re-fueled and to get replenished, so you can get back up and keep on moving forward. I believe in understanding the characteristics of the pit, you will be better prepared to go through this time, and come out on the other side with praise, prayer and purpose. You will be better prepared to recognize depression at its onset, and stop it in its tracks. You will be better equipped to feel emotionally and stay in an atmosphere of connectivity first with God, and then with other people. The more you are able to share with others, the better you will feel about yourself and the things God is taking you through.

Today is the last day you will confess you are depressed. Today is the last day you choose to withdraw. Today is the last day you toy with the thoughts of suicide; never again. Please don't be deceived. You can hear a word like this and get excited and declare you are free, which you are if you confess it, but the enemy is waiting right outside of the door to tempt you with the same thoughts you came in with. The pattern cannot continue and has to be broken. Strongholds are real, and they must be dealt with. The way these things are broken and bound up is when we can truly confess to God where we are. Our lips can praise God, but our heart is far from Him. Some of us are dressed up and making people think we are good, but we are so low in our personal lives that we are not sure if we can handle one more incident. Open up your heart and begin to share where you are with God, and allow Him to come in and heal you from the inside out!

Depression can be defeated when you realize the pit has a purpose; and that purpose is to produce a lifestyle of praise and prayer. As backward as that may sound, I have found it to be true in my life. When a spirit of heaviness tries to knock on the door of my heart, I have trained my soul (my emotions and feelings) to praise the Lord, or to speak of the value that God has in my life. I have learned to open my mouth and communicate with my Father in prayer. And when I pray, I expect God to hear me and to meet my request. And where have I learned to develop these attributes? In the pit of my life; in the place that I felt was inescapable. Where I felt that no one, even the Lord, could help me get out!

I remember laying in the bed feeling miserable about my existence. There was really no reason, nothing out of the extraordinary had happened to me. I was just heavy in my heart-just sad. It was a familiar feeling that I had curiously missed and even slightly welcomed when it presented itself. It was like seeing an old acquaintance-someone I really didn't care to be around, but didn't mind it was there. As I fixed my mind to embrace this blanket of sorrow, something in my spirit shook me and shouted, "No, do not receive this back into your life!" And something caused me to open my mouth and thank God for taking the feeling away. I thanked God for giving me another day to rejoice in Him. I praised the name of Jesus for setting me free from the pit of depression, and somehow, my praises exposed the truth and shed light on the darkness that had so wanted me to embrace it. When I praised God, I placed value on His goodness and devalued the enemy.

Usually when you praise God, praying to Him naturally follows. Once you acknowledge His greatness in your life, you want to talk to the One who loves you so. You want to speak to your Father in heaven and let your requests be made known. That's what happened to me on that morning. After I had praised the Lord, I began to speak to Him. And after I shared how much I appreciated and adored our relationship, I asked God to change my mind and my heart, so I would never again desire to be weighed down with the spirit of heaviness. I asked Him to pour the oil of joy over my life, so I could get moving again. I thanked Him for defeating depression once and for all in my life.

Be sure you thank God for the victory every single day of your life!

Meditation Scriptures

Spiritual Ammunition to Fight Depression

But those who wait on the LORD shall renew their strength; they shall mount up with wings like eagles, they shall run and not be weary, they shall walk and not faint. **Isaiah 40:31**

I shall not die, but live, And declare the works of the LORD. **Psalm 118:17**

I will praise You, for I am fearfully and wonderfully made. Marvelous are Your works, And that my soul knows very well. **Psalm 139:14**

God is our refuge and strength, A very present help in trouble. **Psalm 46:1**

Be anxious for nothing, but in everything by prayer and supplication, with thanksgiving, let your requests be made known to God; **Philippians 4:6**

Be strong and of good courage, do not fear nor be afraid of them; for the LORD your God, He is the One who goes with you. He will not leave you nor forsake you." **Deuteronomy 31:6**

About the Author

Kelley Steele is the Co-Pastor of Kingdom in the Valley Christian Church located in Arizona alongside her husband, Reginald Steele. Over a decade of ministry, teaching, counseling and living out the principles found in God's Word enables her to teach with humor, warmth and strength.

Her message is always straightforward, real and will encourage you in your walk with Christ. She is a wife, mother, author, teacher, conference speaker, recording artist, role model and mentor.

Contact us:

Hunter Heart Publishing
P.O. Box 354
DuPont, Washington 98327

publisher@hunterheartpublishing.com

(253) 906-2160

www.hunterheartpublishing.com

"Offering God's Heart to a Dying World"